Animals I Will Find at the Zoo

KOALA

Shannon Anderson

Table of Contents

A Starfish Book

SEAHORSE PUBLISHING

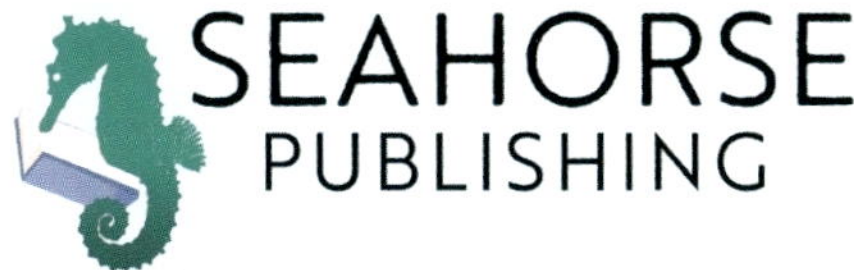

Teaching Tips for Caregivers:

As a caregiver, you can help your child succeed in school by giving them a strong foundation in language and literacy skills and a desire to learn to read.

This book helps children grow by letting them practice reading skills.

Reading for pleasure and interest will help your child to develop reading skills and will give your child the opportunity to practice these skills in meaningful ways.

- Encourage your child to read on her own at home
- Encourage your child to practice reading aloud
- Encourage activities that require reading
- Establish a reading time
- Talk with your child
- Give your child writing materials

Teaching Tips for Teachers:

Research shows that one of the best ways for students to learn a new topic is to read about it.

Before Reading

- Read the "Words to Know" and discuss the meaning of each word.
- Read the back cover to see what the book is about.

During Reading

- When a student gets to a word that is unknown, ask them to look at the rest of the sentence to find clues to help with the meaning of the unknown word.
- Ask the student to write down any pages of the book that were confusing to them.

After Reading

- Discuss the main idea of the book.
- Ask students to give one detail that they learned in the book by showing a text dependent answer from the book.

KOALA

A zoo is a fun place to see animals and learn about them.

One animal you may find in a zoo is a koala.

Koalas may look like teddy bears.

But they are not bears at all.

Koalas are **mammals** called **marsupials**.

Marsupials are animals that have pouches on their bodies.

They carry their babies inside the pouches.

Baby koalas are called **joeys**.

Joeys are about the size of a jelly bean when they are born.

They have no fur.

They cannot see or hear yet.

When a joey is born, it climbs into its mom's pouch.

Joeys live there for about six months.

When joeys get too big for the pouch, they ride on their mom's back.

Later, they learn to climb in the trees.

Koalas have strong arms and legs for climbing trees.

Their big claws help them dig into tree trunks.

Koalas have two thumbs on each front paw.

Koalas sleep 18 to 20 hours each day.

When they are not sleeping, they are often eating.

There are 24 hours in one day.

A koala’s favorite food is **eucalyptus** leaves.

These leaves harm other animals, but not koalas.

Adult koalas can eat one pound (one-half kilogram) of leaves a day.

NORTH AMERICA
EUROPE
ASIA
AFRICA
SOUTH AMERICA
AUSTRALIA

Koalas live in **Australia**.

If you cannot go to Australia to see koalas, you can find them at the zoo!

Words to Know

Australia (aw-STRAIL-yuh): one of Earth's continents; the continent that is south and east of Asia

eucalyptus (yoo-kuh-LIP-tuhs): a tall evergreen tree found mostly in Australia

joeys (JOH-eez): baby koalas

mammals (MAM-uhlz): animals that have hair or fur, that give birth to live babies, and that make milk to feed their babies

marsupials (mahr-SOO-pee-ulz): animals that carry their babies in pouches on their abdomens

Index

Comprehension Questions

1. Koalas are from ____.
   a. Europe b. South America c. Australia

2. What kind of animals are koalas?
   a. reptiles b. kangaroos c. marsupials

3. Baby koalas are called ___.
   a. joeys b. jills c. jelly beans

4. True or False: Baby koalas live in their mother's pouch for two years.

5. True or False: Koalas sleep most of the day.

Answers
1. c 2. c 3. a 4. False 5. True

About the Author

Shannon Anderson is an award-winning children's book author and former elementary school teacher. She loves animals and has eight pets of her own. You can learn more about her or invite her to your school at www.shannonisteaching.com.

Written by: Shannon Anderson
Design by: Under the Oaks Media
Editor: Kim Thompson

Library of Congress PCN Data
Koala / Shannon Anderson
Animals I Will Find at the Zoo
ISBN 979-8-8873-5349-4 (hard cover)
ISBN 979-8-8873-5434-7 (paperback)
ISBN 979-8-8873-5519-1 (EPUB)
ISBN 979-8-8873-5604-4 (eBook)
Library of Congress Control Number: 2022949067

Printed in the United States of America.

Photographs/Shutterstock: slowmotiongli: cover; white jellybeans: p. 3, 20; Japan's Fireworks: p. 5; EQRoy: p. 6; YellowCat: p. 8; Carla Thomas: p. 9; Worldswildlifesonders: p. 10; AlizadaStudios: p. 12; Lucie Lang: p. 13; Marianne Purdie: p. 15; Bildagentur Zoonar Gmbh: p. 16; Chris de Blank: p. 17; Cozine: p. 18-19; photofortz7: p. 19; Pyty: p. 20(map); dan_locke: p. 21

Seahorse Publishing Company
www.seahorsepub.com

Published in the United States
Seahorse Publishing
PO Box 771325
Coral Springs, FL 33077